Fine Home
Contracting

Finding, Fixing, and
Funding Your Dream Home
or Investment Property

David Perrotti

Editor: Shannon Buritz
Published by Remarkable Press
Copyright © 2021 by David Perrotti

David Perrotti-- 1st ed.

ISBN: 978-1-954757-00-4
The Publisher has strived to be as accurate and complete as possible in the creation of this book.

This book is not intended for use as a legal, business, accounting, or financial advice source. All readers are advised to seek the services of competent professionals in legal, business, accounting, and finance fields.

Like anything else in life, there are no guarantees of income or results in practical advice books. Readers are cautioned to rely on their judgment about their individual circumstances to act accordingly.

While all attempts have been made to verify information provided in this publication, the Publisher assumes no responsibility for errors, omissions, or contrary interpretation of the subject matter herein. Any perceived slights of specific persons, peoples, or organizations are unintentional.

CONTENTS

INTRODUCTION

Do you want to turn an old house into your home? Perhaps you love the house's historic feel but dream about making it "your own" with restorations and cosmetic updates. You probably have many questions and fears, such as…

- Is renovation right for me?
- Will it be costly and complicated?
- Am I capable of hiring a large team and helping to make decisions about the home of my dreams?
- Will the project be over budget, over schedule, and ultimately, a money pit?

Don't allow these fears to hold you back from the gratifying experience of renovating your home into a place for you and your family to grow and thrive for years to come. Renovation lending is the most straightforward, cost-effective path to reach your final goal. Allow me to guide you through the process from start to finish as we discuss loan options, choosing the right team of professionals, and what to expect along the way. I'll discuss common mistakes and things to avoid to save you valuable time and energy. With this book as your guide, the home you envision is just within reach. Let me take you there.

David Perrotti

Want Our Help?

Claim Your Complimentary "Vision Session" Today!

At Your Vision Session, You Will Discover:

- The best ways to finance your project
- A detailed review of your dream by a highly-trained consultant
- Brainstorming solutions for your project needs
- How we can help you with your dream
- Remodeling industry knowledge shared
- Solutions that fit your "why"

This valuable session is a consultation, not a sales pitch.

Schedule Your Complimentary "Vision Session" at:
www.finehomecontracting.com/book

CHAPTER ONE

Renovation Loans...A Smarter Choice

magine finding the home of your dreams. It is in a great neighborhood with schools, parks, and amenities close by. All it requires is some upgrading to make it to your specific style and functionality needs. Perhaps you love your current home and would like to refinance to complete some remodeling projects. In either case, a renovation loan is by far the cheapest and smartest way to remodel. There is little money out of pocket, and all renovations can be financed with very low-interest rates. Not to mention, since it is a government-backed loan, you can leverage a lot of remodeling power that you wouldn't typically have, and the interest on the loan is tax-deductible!

Let's begin with using a renovation loan for a new home purchase. In the Northeast, where I am located, most houses are 30 years or older. New home buyers will be purchasing homes that will undoubtedly need remodeled kitchens, bathrooms, or exterior replacement of roof, windows, and siding. As the buyer, you want that particular style, a new kitchen with an open floor plan, granite countertops, a steam shower, or a maintenance-free exterior. But who has that kind of cash right after purchasing a home? You can have it all with one renovation loan. Renovation loans allow you to buy any home based on location and then renovate it with all the details to create your dream home. This is especially beneficial in a seller's market. The best part is, you don't even have to move in until all the work is done because many lenders will roll the first couple of mortgage payments right into the loan. You aren't inconvenienced by the dust, noise, and disruption that goes hand in hand with remodeling. Just make sure you can stay in your existing residence for a couple of extra months until the work is complete. Then you get that incredible feeling of moving into your dream house, which typically only happens when going with the costly option of having a custom home built.

Renovation loans are also the best route from an investment perspective. There is a lot of data out there about the return on a remodeling project, and you certainly don't get a 100% return. Let's use remodeling your kitchen as an example. You are going to spend $50,000 on this project. If you were to put cash in, your money would be gone. You would only get about $40,000 back based on zip code and current market value. So you would lose $10,000 right off the bat, and all of that money would be tied up. If you had used a renovation loan and ended up selling after only a few years of completing the work, you would have only paid a couple of thousand dollars in additional mortgage payments. When you go to sell, you get that 80% equity back, and you only ended up spending $5,000 or $6,000 on a kitchen that you got to live with and enjoy. Upon selling, your house is now worth more.

Similarly, renovation loans can be used to refinance. Maybe you have been in your house for a while, and the entire exterior needs to be done, including a roof, windows, and siding. Or maybe your in-laws are moving in, and you want to build an in-law suite. Sure, you have a nice nest egg set aside, but you don't want to use that. With a renovation loan, you can refinance and roll all of it into a new mortgage with low-interest rates. You can complete all of the desired work, and you may find that your monthly payment is the same with today's current lower 3% interest rates. Traditionally, people have used a home equity line of credit for repairs and renovations on their home. The beautiful thing about a renovation loan is that you don't need equity in your home because the loan is based on future equity that the renovation will create. The calculations are based on the "after improved" value of the house. This is beneficial, especially if you have been in your home a few short years and have only $10,000 of equity built up. You can't do much with $10,000. But let's say you want to put on a $300,000 addition. The loan will be evaluated based on that project's future value and allows way more flexibility than other finance forms. With interest rates being so low, it's basically "free money" and will enable you to keep your cash stashed away securely for the future needs of your family.

Finding the Renovation Loan That Works for You

There are a few to choose from, including FHA, Fannie Mae, Freddie Mac, and VA when it comes to renovation loans. Each of these loans is (technically) taxpayer-backed, so essentially, we are all subsidizing them. This enables more accessibility to the public and keeps rates down. Each type of loan caters to a different market.

FHA is a first time home buyer loan with a lower credit score requirement and less money down. Fannie Mae needs a higher credit score and often more money down. Freddie Mac falls somewhere in between the two. Finally, the VA loan is specifically for veterans. Most commonly used are the FHA 203K and the Fannie Mae Homestyle loans. The majority of lenders will be very familiar with these because they tend to encompass the largest part of the population.

The FHA 203K allows you to begin the process with a lower credit score and package everything together into a low down payment. It is broken into two parts, the "limited" and the "standard." The limited is any amount below $35,000, while the standard is above $35,000. A standard FHA 203K will be different in that it requires a HUD consultant. A HUD consultant is an inspector who protects the government and lenders to make sure that work is being done correctly and to code before paying the contractor. A benefit of the FHA 203k program is that the loan can be up to 110% of the property value, which works out well in more urban areas where the house might not appraise out but requires a lot of work because it is in poor condition. This makes it a popular option for homes in larger cities and towns.

The FHA 203k has a set of guidelines called "health and safety items." These items must be taken care of first, before any desired renovations. Essentially, the home needs to be habitable. There is a 35 point checklist, including intact siding, operational windows and doors, functioning utilities, railings and appliances that don't present tripping hazards. Lead paint and asbestos issues also must be remedied. Many times, much of the budget can be eaten up on these. That is the trade-off for the 110% appraisal value. Once the required items are taken care of on the repair list, you can then move on to your wishlist items. If you want to upgrade that kitchen...now is the time! The only limitation with this type of loan is luxury items. It cannot be used for swimming pools, whirlpools, etc. If you find yourself daydreaming about these additions to your home, the next loan we will discuss would be a match.

As mentioned above, the Fannie Mae Homestyle does require a higher credit score but also offers low-interest rates. Health and safety items are cut in half with this type of loan, and you can use it to finance those luxury items. We see this loan used a lot when it comes to refinancing. For example, let's say you built a deck way back in the day and didn't install proper railings. You have been living with it, enjoying life on it, and it isn't a concern for you. If you choose to finance through an FHA loan, the consultant will come in and tell you that the railings must be added before completing your wish-list items. The Fannie Mae Homestyle loan is much more flexible when it comes to health and safety. Also, if you want to put that big pool in, you can spend $100,000, as long as the appraisal numbers work out. You can do anything and everything, as long as you are not over-improving for your area. In other words, you can't renovate to a $300,000 value in a $200,000 neighborhood.

Between the FHA 203K and the Fannie Mae Homestyle, there is something for everyone. They do a great job of fulfilling the needs of most buyers in the market. Keep in mind that each lender is different, and things are changing all the time. There is a misconception that renovation loans are complicated because many lenders simply don't understand the process. Working with an experienced team of professionals will keep you armed with the knowledge to make informed decisions about the right loan. When your realtor, lender, and contractor are well versed in renovation lending, all you have to worry about is choosing your favorite colors, flooring, or other items that will transform your dreams into reality.

Want Our Help?

Claim Your Complimentary "Vision Session" Today!

At Your Vision Session, You Will Discover:

- The best ways to finance your project
- A detailed review of your dream by a highly-trained consultant
- Brainstorming solutions for your project needs
- How we can help you with your dream
- Remodeling industry knowledge shared
- Solutions that fit your "why"

This valuable session is a consultation, not a sales pitch.

Schedule Your Complimentary
"Vision Session" at:
www.finehomecontracting.com/book

CHAPTER TWO

Finding the Right Lender/Realtor Team

The lender and the realtor are the two most important people when getting your new home to the closing table. Working with professionals with a high level of experience will make the entire process fast, easy, and stress-free. Take your time to find the lender/realtor team that gives you confidence and is armed with the knowledge to help you make one of the most significant purchases of your life.

What to Look for in a Lender

There is a lot that goes into the renovation lending process and just buying a home in general. Nothing beats an experienced lender as they know what to look for and all the variables that come into play. It is a large transaction with a lot of moving pieces. If the lender is unfamiliar with the renovation loan component, they will undoubtedly get lost and, consequently, lose the home of your dreams in the process. Often, we see buyers two months into the process when all of a sudden, the deal falls through because the lender didn't understand how to do the proper paperwork. The buyer has now wasted all of this time searching for the home and spent thousands of dollars on inspections, only to be left frustrated and back at square one. By choosing a lender well-versed in renovation loans, you save yourself time and money and can achieve the ultimate goal of making it to the closing table.

There are many brokerage companies out there. These brokerages get connected with wholesale departments of more prominent lenders, and they sell the loans. Essentially, they are just packaging the loans. The more prominent companies, on the other hand, do everything in house. We refer to these as "servicers," which is where we encourage people to go for lending. They are packaging, servicing, and underwriting that loan all in one spot.

Also, they perform the service of the renovation portion too. It is imperative that the file starts and ends in the same building, with the actual draws and payments for the renovation coming from the same company. We often find with small brokers that a month into the process, when it hits the second tier of underwriting, it gets kicked back. This is typically a result of a lack of experience since all they are doing is packaging the loan and selling it wholesale. Even if you have a good friend or family member who is a broker and want to give them your business, you have to consider if it will be worth your time and frustration. Make sure to ask the crucial questions to your lender, such as, "Are you keeping this in house? Are you selling it? Who are you going to sell it to?" We ask these questions all the time. If it ends up being one of the big companies that we've worked with, we will go ahead and push it through. We know the back end, how it will get through processing, and the reputation of the company.

It all goes back to knowing the process well enough to anticipate what is needed before something will delay or destroy the deal. A good loan officer will evaluate the property through a pre-appraisal, look at the neighborhood, work the numbers in their head, and have a pretty good idea if it will all work out. The loan officer needs to understand the renovation process and be able to confidently say, "If we put $100,000 into this house, it will appraise out." If this ballpark appraisal doesn't happen first, the real appraiser will arrive at the end of the process and determine the house is way overvalued for the neighborhood. At this point, everything is shut down, and the deal falls through. By then, so much time has been wasted.

It also helps to have the underwriting team in house. Underwriting has the daunting job of putting all the paperwork together for analysis. When you're doing a renovation loan, you're also adding a lot of additional paperwork. There is the contract, work scope, material and labor, and write-ups from the HUD consultants or home inspectors. The underwriters need to understand terminology, the construction process, and health and safety issues. Companies that specialize in renovations loans have a much smoother underwriting process. Nothing gets held up due to questions like "What does this mean?" and you proceed to that closing table in no time.

After the loan has closed, it's not over. The renovation still has to be paid for by the draw department of the lending company. We have experienced issues with the draw departments on the contracting side with many lenders. When dealing with a company that sells the loan, that loan often ends up in the middle of nowhere, between companies. We ask to get paid because the work is already complete, and the file is missing. Keeping it in house allows the contractor to get in quick and start working immediately upon closing. It also ensures they will get paid promptly and not walk off the job when payment is not readily available. The contractor needs money to keep everything going and will have no choice but to walk if the draw department is inexperienced. Some of the best companies we have worked for set up direct deposit directly to our account, allowing us to get those jobs done twice as fast. By doing some simple internet research, you can find lenders who demonstrate expertise in renovation lending by providing thorough information on their websites. The more knowledge and writing about the process online, the better your chances become of getting into your desired home.

What to Look for in a Realtor

Renovation loans have been around for 20 to 30 years. Even so, realtors typically want to shy away from them because the probability of the deal going through goes down. There are more hurdles they have to jump through, such as additional paperwork and dealing with contractors. Keep in mind that realtors work on volume, so they want to get that house to closing, be done with it, and move on to the next. So finding the right realtor can be challenging. You want someone who has not only done renovation loans in the past but is still open to doing them for you and sharing your vision. Vision is essential when it comes to choosing a realtor. You want someone who can walk through a home with you and say things like, "Wow, we can open this wall up to expand the kitchen and add new flooring here. Look at the house next door. You have a lot of room to move up." The realtor should be willing and able to help you find the right neighborhood to complement the desired renovations. Remember that a house can be altered to your wants and needs, but a community can't. First, choose the neighborhood based on schools, proximity to family, entertainment, and amenities. If you find an imperfect house in that perfect neighborhood, you always have the power to make changes to the house. A realtor that understands the process and a little bit about remodeling is the perfect match. They should encourage you to look past what the house needs and dream about what it "could be."

When it comes to writing the offer, it isn't much different than a typical real estate transaction, which is a common misconception among realtors. They just have to annotate that it will be a renovation loan and understand the negotiation's remodeling components. Any good realtor knows how to negotiate. The contractor will provide a write up stating how much money they will put into the home, which will give the realtor a good negotiation starting point.

Like loan officers, realtors have a low barrier to entry, meaning it doesn't take a long time to get a license. So there are many part-time realtors out there that only do five or six transactions a year. You want a realtor that does 20 or 30 transactions a year, which is a good indicator of experience. Ideally, the perfect realtor will have renovation loan and remodeling knowledge, share your vision, value what you want, and get the deal done.

Knowing Where to Begin

When you have decided that you want a fixer-upper, what is the first step? Do you head out right away and start looking at properties? We highly recommend that you first find a lender with renovation loan experience. The lender is going to start you with a budget. Let's say the most they can get you on loan is $300,000. Now you know to look at houses in the $200,000 - $300,000 range (obviously on the lower end of that if the property needs work). The next step is to find a realtor that can take you directly to homes in that price range, saving a lot of time. From there, you can get quotes from a contractor on the scope of work and exact amounts needed to complete it.

Often we see people start the process backward. They drive around neighborhoods and set their hearts on the house first. Maybe they have a $200,000 budget, and they find a home at that price in a $500,000 neighborhood. They get very excited, thinking they have just found a great deal. What they don't know without working with a lender/realtor first is that the home is a foreclosure, and it is valued at $200,000 because it needs $300,000 worth of work. As contractors, we see this happen often. They decide they can afford $250,000 at the most and think that an extra $50,000 will cover the cost of repairing the septic well, the new kitchen, the modern bathroom, and the mold problem in the basement. By having a professional team in place first, you won't get too far in over your head and end up with heartache when you discover it won't work out as you initially hoped.

As a contractor, we offer mini home inspections. If you happen to find a home on your own, we can come out, walk you through it and explain the costs. We can even look through reports and other resources to identify any health and safety issues that need to be taken care of before desired renovations. As far as the remodeling side, we have many excellent handouts that are broken down into tiers. For example, if you wanted to remodel the kitchen, we can show you three different finishes and pricing levels to know what to expect. Then we can guide you to a great lender and realtor from there. By seeking out an experienced team of professionals to share in your vision and guide you through the process, your new home is just within reach.

Want Our Help?

Claim Your Complimentary "Vision Session" Today!

At Your Vision Session, You Will Discover:

- The best ways to finance your project
- A detailed review of your dream by a highly-trained consultant
- Brainstorming solutions for your project needs
- How we can help you with your dream
- Remodeling industry knowledge shared
- Solutions that fit your "why"

This valuable session is a consultation, not a sales pitch.

Schedule Your Complimentary "Vision Session" at:
www.finehomecontracting.com/book

CHAPTER THREE

The Essential Role of the Contractor

Finding an experienced contractor is a vital piece of the renovation puzzle. After all, they are the company managing, scheduling, and performing the physical labor involved in creating your future home. You want a contractor on time, on budget, and on schedule to meet your expectations and allow you to move in as soon as possible. In Connecticut and several other states, the barrier to entry for a contractor is relatively low. They go through a registration process and pay $250, which doesn't sound like quite enough considering all of the crucial tasks the contractor is responsible for. "Licensed and insured" is more of a buzzword and will not help you screen out a good contractor. Of course, you want to work with one that is licensed and insured. But since the licensing is relatively easy to obtain, you need to dig a little deeper to ensure a reputable company.

How to Find the Right Contractor

A good starting point is through word of mouth. Ask your network of friends and neighbors if they have had remodeling projects done and who they used. If possible, take a look at the actual work performed and ask how the overall experience was. But don't stop there. Even the worst contractors get lucky and do decent work now and then. After you have a few names, begin doing your online research. Look at websites, reviews, and whether or not the company specializes in renovation loans. Are there price guides? Are they explaining their systems well? Do they provide blog posts and examples pertaining to your specific project? The more information provided, the better.

If you start a Google search with no referrals, excellent search terms are "FHA 203K contractor" or "general contractors near me." Google will give you the map and a list of the organic reach, as well as ads. Take a look at the ads since these will provide you with a good idea of specialization. Choose three or four contractors that appeal to you. They should have websites with extensive information, attractive photos, and a way to reach out and message the sales team or project manager. Take those names and enter each one in a Google search individually. Google will then populate everywhere the contractor's name pops up. You will have full access to reviews and information on Houzz, Angie's List, Porch, HomeAdvisor, the Better Business Bureau, and any Chambers of Commerce they are members of.

Social media presence is another strong indicator of an experienced contractor. The good guys will be shameless and transparent on social media because they do an excellent job, stand behind their work, don't want any negative reviews, and are open to having people directly message them. The contractors that are hiding are the ones to be concerned about.

Once you have a nice list with reliable reviews and an online presence, it is time to make some phone calls. To screen contractors effectively, start by telling them about your specific project and see what their response is. Then make sure to ask the following questions:

- What size is the company? (Is there a project manager, sales team, or just one person wearing all the hats?)

- Are there processes in place for running a project? (Is there a schedule, budget, and backup in case a project manager or subcontractor gets sick to ensure timely completion?)

- What kind of warranties do they have on their services? (Do they provide a one-year follow up to make sure everything was done correctly and work is still up to specs?)

- What do they specialize in? (If you want an addition and they mostly deal with bathroom remodels, it may not be a good fit.)

- Are they members of any associations? (Organizations like The HBRA - Home Builders and Remodelers Association and NARI - National Association of the Remodeling Industry, provide the latest training, classes, and information to their members. Most reputable contractors will proudly display their membership to these associations. We recently received excellent training on Covid best practices on the construction site. Membership in these groups keeps us educated, informed of new codes, and updated on new materials used in the industry.)

Specializations

When it comes to specializations, there is a wide variety. We have coined my company, particularly as a "general contracting management company," emphasizing the management piece. We hire whoever is needed for the specific project. We are excellent at finding them, screening them, creating expectations, and managing the money so that subcontractors don't walk away. We specialize in the management of multi-faceted projects, which makes us an ideal choice for renovations. As opposed to a contractor who might only specialize in kitchens, we can handle projects with kitchens, bathrooms, additions, septic work, roofing, driveways, tree removal - you name it.

Over the years, each trade has become more complex, making it necessary to bring in different groups of people for each portion of a renovation project. Installing a tile shower, for example, is a week-long certification process requiring specialized training, tools, and materials. When we took a look at the industry, we realized that there was no shortage of people that could do good work. But nobody was concentrating on the most significant lacking factor in the industry, which is management. With one phone call to us, we will have a salesperson to your home in 24 hours, spending time to go over your wants and needs, problem-solving, and then handing your project to an experienced team of professionals that we hand select to complete the work. We pride ourselves on organizing and funding the entire project, which results in satisfied, stress-free clients.

The Benefits of Working with A Sales Team

A contractor with a salesperson or team should always be chosen over one without. This is an indicator of a highly structured company and ensures that you will not get price gouged. When a salesperson comes to meet you, there is a price book somewhere in the background. Pre-determined prices for each portion of your project already exist, eliminating the possibility of a contractor overcharging and pocketing the extra cash. The salesperson benefits from the sale, so they want it to make sense. They must systematically and accurately put together pricing so that they can hand it off to somebody else who gets the job produced. If something were exaggerated, the project manager would question the additional surplus of funds. Choosing a contractor with a sales department keeps your money safe.

It is a common misconception that smaller companies will have less overhead and, therefore, cheaper prices. In reality, larger companies will have a designated person working on estimating and making sure pricing is up to date. This person will devote much of their time shopping for many products and services to keep the company efficient and reasonably priced. The bigger the company, the more resources and people they will have to focus on materials and whether they have the very best subcontractors. Also, larger contractors get work done more quickly and efficiently. If you have one guy that sells, does the work, and does the bookkeeping, how will the project ever reach completion? We are always monitoring months ahead and have levers that we flip if we anticipate things starting to get hectic. For example, we might hire an additional project manager if we reach an inevitable production overload. Within reason, a contractor should have the scalability to expand the workforce when needed to complete your home within the scheduled time frame.

The Relationship

Many people may not realize that the relationship with your contractor is one of the most intimate of any hire you make. When you go to the doctor, you're only there for an hour. He pokes and prods you, and then you are on your merry way. You might see him again in another year. When you hire a contractor for a big remodeling project, they will be at your house for a long time. If it is a refinance situation with a remodel and you will be staying in the house, these guys will be hanging out with your kids and your dog inside your home for months. You don't just randomly pick anyone to be in your house for six months, every single day. A remodel is exceptionally stressful. Even though we are great at what we do, by month four, when things are 70% complete, and we are waiting on special order items, paint, or drywall, the homeowners are ready to be done with disruption in their lives. This is always a great time to send our production manager in with a bottle of wine, letting the client know that we understand how they feel and how ready they are for the dust to clear and the workers to go home. Throw a BAD contractor into the mix, and the stress level intensifies tenfold. They don't clean up after themselves, leave and don't tell you when they are coming back, or they don't show up at all.

Take your time when choosing your contractor. Don't underestimate the commitment, skill, communication, and organization it takes for them to get you settled into your completed home. By obtaining referrals, doing your research, and screening companies with the strategies offered in this chapter, you will be able to make an informed, confident decision to meet your renovation needs.

Want Our Help?

Claim Your Complimentary "Vision Session" Today!

At Your Vision Session, You Will Discover:

- The best ways to finance your project
- A detailed review of your dream by a highly-trained consultant
- Brainstorming solutions for your project needs
- How we can help you with your dream
- Remodeling industry knowledge shared
- Solutions that fit your "why"

This valuable session is a consultation, not a sales pitch.

Schedule Your Complimentary "Vision Session" at:
www.finehomecontracting.com/book

CHAPTER FOUR

Finding the Ideal House

Choosing the right fixer-upper requires a little bit of vision on your part. Try to look at the property's potential rather than the "as-is" state of the house. Remember that you cannot change location and lot size, so these need to be some of the first boxes checked. If you have children, research the school district. Decide if you will have enough yard space and privacy to keep you satisfied with the home long after the renovations are complete.

Neighborhood

There are many factors to consider when it comes to neighborhood selection. Not only do you want to consider things like sidewalks, schools, and amenities, you also want to take into consideration the appraised value of the surrounding houses. For example, let's say you buy a home for $200,000 in a $200,000 neighborhood. If you plan on putting $100,000 worth of work into the house, it will never appraise out. If you are going to put that kind of time, money, and effort into a property, you need to be sure the neighborhood can hold the value. Here in Connecticut, we have streets with homes ranging in value from $300,000 to 4 or 5 million. Communities like these with a "high end" will make it easier for you to improve without restrictions.

When choosing your neighborhood, it is imperative to have the right realtor and loan officer in place. They can steer you toward areas with upward mobility to ensure things work out on the appraisal side. At the same time, they are knowledgeable about amenities, school systems, and other elements that may be important to you and your family. A skilled team will ensure that your renovation efforts add value in the long run.

Vacant Properties and Foreclosures

When you are looking at a house that is either a foreclosure or has been vacant for a while, the biggest culprit for deals falling through is a septic on the property. If nobody has been using it, then it is tough to test. We recommend that you go into it knowing that a septic costs between $15,000 and $20,000 and plan for the worst. Make sure you include the very real possibility of a new septic system in your budget. The same applies to a well. Many times, the power is off, and well and septic cannot be tested. Septic and wells in rural areas can blow your budget if you can't get them tested and don't anticipate the added costs.

Another thing to be aware of is the issue of additions and septic. Depending on where your septic fields are, you can only build within so many feet of them. If you are adding X amount of space, the septic may not handle the house's additional occupants. Your building permits will not be approved if your septic is too small for your project to extend the house.

If you are walking into a project with city sewer, water, and gas hookups, your probability of making successful improvements increases significantly. Here in Connecticut, many of the houses are old, and the septic systems are reaching their life expectancy. It is a big-ticket item, as a brand new engineered system can be $50,000. As far as wells, if you are not getting enough water out of it, you automatically won't be eligible for certain financing/mortgages. If you have your heart set on a property with well and septic, examine and budget for those areas first before moving on to your new kitchen or maintenance-free exterior.

Vision

Having a vision for the remodel and upgrades can be overwhelming for buyers. Being in the industry, I take it for granted to see a house for what it "could be." All you have to do is turn on HGTV to gain some clarity on how to think outside the box when it comes to the fixer-upper dauntingly staring you in the face. You can start by only focusing on the layout of the home. Look at where you can add rooms and take down walls. Maybe you don't like the kitchen, but a simple wall removal can create the open concept you are looking for. Finishing a basement or adding an addition can offer more living space. You have to go into it thinking this way, but also make sure the house has the ability to make those things work. A walk-through with your realtor and contractor helps know whether these visions can come to fruition. Do keep in mind that the core of the house should match your size and style requirements. For example, you can't change a colonial-style house into a contemporary one. You want to like the "bones" of the home and simply make personal touches on items like bathrooms, kitchens, paint, and flooring.

During the vision stage, it is also essential to understand what anticipated costs will be. Don't ask your uncle how much his water heater was or your neighbor what they paid for their kitchen remodel. You need to research real data online that provides cost by zip code. My company offers a "cost versus value" handout, breaking down the price of each project. This is very helpful when you can go into the desired home and say to yourself, "This house needs a kitchen which will run between $30,000 and $60,000, and a bathroom for around $25,000." You can then determine if the house is already overpriced or if it won't appraise out appropriately. Knowledge is power for making the house exactly what you want while still being able to afford the final price. Working with an experienced loan officer will give you a good idea of what you can afford on a monthly mortgage payment and how much remodeling budget you will have to work with. If you have been approved for $300,000 and are looking at a $200,000 home, you can feel confident knowing that your $100,000 renovation budget can cover that new kitchen and HVAC system. Having these big-ticket items priced out is an essential first step, and then we can move on to helping you choose finish types and knowing what to expect cost-wise. We typically use Pinterest to help customers create a board with desired finishes such as tile versus linoleum, hardwood versus carpet, etc. Those items will get you to your price point as well. There is some excellent information on the internet but remember always to get costs based on your specific zip code. Various parts of the country differ dramatically in labor costs. Here in the Northeast, even material costs and cost of living are incredibly high.

Remodeling will naturally be a lot more expensive here than in the Midwest or South. Do this research with a contractor beforehand, and get data from more than one contractor since that one contractor may not know what they are talking about. The industry standard uses that data to keep you safe and guarantee that the project reaches completion. A good contractor will make those things happen.

The Benefits of a Home Cost Analysis

For a nominal fee, a member of our sales team can take off their sales hat to sit down with you and analyze what you are trying to achieve with your fixer-upper. They will provide you with a list of cost breakdowns and desired outcomes to determine whether you want to purchase the home. If you have already made the purchase, the Home Cost Analysis can help you decide what you can improve within your particular budget. Since our salesperson is being compensated for being a consultant, they will spend the time with you to create the best possible solutions based on your long-term goals for the house. How long are you going to stay there? Who will be living in the home? What are you trying to accomplish? How much wear and tear do you expect? Do you have pets? All of these questions can help determine what types of materials and finishes are best suited for your family. On the buyer's side, the Home Cost Analysis is a powerful negotiation tool that you can present to the seller when discussing the home's necessary work. If you choose our company to complete the renovations for you, the Home Cost Analysis is fully refunded.

Refinancing Your Current Home with a Renovation Loan

Most people don't think about renovation loans for refinancing. Especially now, with today's market and the interest rates being low, it is a perfect opportunity. Maybe you have been in your home for 20-30 years, and everything is looking dated. Or perhaps you bought it when it was already in need of updating. So now it's really dated. Maybe it is just deferred maintenance at this point. In cases like these, even if you don't plan on living there much longer, it makes sense to come in, refinance, and renovate for a quicker, more profitable sale. You will end up with a lot more value in your home and a higher asking price. Even though it may not be your first thought, a renovation loan is the best way to refinance your current home. The mortgage process is smoother, you can take more time, and there is no pressure of your house being on the market having deadlines to meet. We push this with any customer that calls wanting renovations. We ask them if they have thought about refinancing and if their mortgage is at a higher interest rate. We let them know that our referral partners can help them get their monthly mortgage payment down, all while putting in that new dream kitchen. It is always fun to hear the excitement from customers who didn't even realize this was attainable. Since there is no stress caused by underwriting and closing where things typically go awry, the probability of these loans going through is significantly higher.

When it comes to refinancing, the Fannie Mae Homestyle loan is used much more frequently than other options. Their health and safety requirements are much lower than the FHA 203K. For example, if you have a deck built by your uncle, and the railing system wasn't done correctly, an FHA 203K would require those railings to be replaced. The Fannie Mae Homestyle allows most things to remain unchanged that you have been living with contentedly.

The renovation loan process essentially follows the same path with either loan you choose. You start with an inspection and walk through with your contractor, come up with a scope of work, material, and labor costs, and finally, the contractor gets vetted by the bank. Once the refinance loan closes, the money becomes available in escrow, and the work begins. The contractor receives progress payments; as one project gets done, an inspector comes out to ensure completion, and the lender releases the payments accordingly. At the end of the project, everything gets closed out, and you have a beautifully updated home with lower monthly payments!

Other forms of financing simply won't give you the power of the renovation loan. People sometimes opt for a home equity line of credit, but that only allows you to draw upon the current equity. A renovation loan looks at the future value of the home after the renovations are complete. If you plan a $200,000 addition that will add $200,000 of value to the house, that amount is applied to the new loan. Most people simply do not have enough equity on their own to complete all of their desired projects, and it puts limits on what they can do.

A "cash-out" refinance is another option where you get money back at closing that can be used for remodeling purposes. Again, this amount will be based on how much equity you have in your home. This puts you at a disadvantage if you have only been in your home for a few years.

Lastly, people choose to use the zero percent, unsecured credit lines like what you see at Home Depot or other big box stores. Unfortunately, these come with very high-interest rates and a short term, typically ten years maximum. As you can see, there is no other refinance option on the market that will give you low monthly payments and incredible buying power based on future equity. Using a renovation loan for your current home is a win-win!

You Can do It...With the Right Team!

Creating the home of your dreams can be an overwhelming endeavor. Don't underestimate how easy it can be with the right team of professionals in place. With limited resources upfront, you can bring your visions to life with a renovation loan. As a stressed-out mom, you can finally have that spa bathroom. As an aspiring cook, you can create that gourmet kitchen. Don't allow your nerves about the process to interfere with making those dreams a reality. We always recommend browsing sites like Pinterest and Houzz to find inspiration and possibilities. Though HGTV is a little skewed on their scheduling and pricing, the home shows can give you excellent tips and ideas. Especially in areas like here in the Northeast, most of the land has already been built on. And if you want that custom home, you will need to renovate and create it from an already existing one. In the current pandemic environment, people are spending more and more time in their homes. Now more than ever, we can't let the fear of something going wrong hold us back from creating home office spaces, e-learning areas, or simply more room for our families to enjoy. Again, a lot of that fear and uncertainty can be alleviated with a Home Cost Analysis. Our experts can talk to you about the house's flow, load-bearing walls, and things that can or cannot be torn out easily. During this analysis, we digitize your home into a 3D rendering. You can play around with elements like windows, siding, color, and texture on the exterior. We then use other software to allow for similar customization on the inside of the home. It produces all of the square footage and linear feet so that our team can give you the most accurate pricing on your desired renovations. We provide you with a full report to easily make a decision that you can feel good about. It is very powerful to see your ideas take shape in digital form and keep your focus on the end goal...the home that will be the envy of the neighborhood!

Want Our Help?

Claim Your Complimentary "Vision Session" Today!

At Your Vision Session, You Will Discover:

- The best ways to finance your project
- A detailed review of your dream by a highly-trained consultant
- Brainstorming solutions for your project needs
- How we can help you with your dream
- Remodeling industry knowledge shared
- Solutions that fit your "why"

This valuable session is a consultation, not a sales pitch.

Schedule Your Complimentary "Vision Session" at:
www.finehomecontracting.com/book

CHAPTER FIVE

The Ins and Outs of Inspections

Whether you are buying or refinancing a home, there is a required inspection. The inspector will create a report detailing the general deficiencies of the house and health and safety issues. When using an FHA 203K loan, this entire list needs to be addressed and accounted for in the renovation portion. It ends up looking a lot like the Wild West out there because many of these items are subjective. It is crucial to use a HUD inspector during this process. With their additional licensing requirements and education, HUD inspectors are one step above standard home inspectors and are always used with FHA 203K loans.

Based on their findings, the HUD inspector will determine what permits are necessary for your scope of work. Their primary responsibility is to protect the lender and the government from contractors and homeowners taking the money and putting it into things other than property improvements. The allotted money must go towards work on the home. If something were to happen down the road, such as a foreclosure, the house would be taken back, and the improvements will already have been made to the property. The bank is made whole at that point.

The Process

After the HUD inspector comes up with the list of required items, they will work with the contractor on your wish list items, such as that new kitchen or updated bathroom. From there, the inspector will create a "feasibility report." This report details what everything should cost and acts as a protection to the homeowner so the contractor cannot price gouge. The HUD inspector provides this report to the contractor, leaving the pricing blank to ensure the contractor comes within a similar range. If the pricing matches up appropriately, the HUD inspector will sign off and adjust their numbers to meet the contractors.

Whenever the loan is a full FHA 203K, above $35,000, or needing structural repairs, a HUD inspector is required. They are compensated each time they come out to do an inspection. They will take pictures, inspect the work, make sure you have proper permits, and then create a draw request for each percentage of the work completed. The buyer will review the photos and the report of finished work and sign off, at which point the HUD inspector submits this report to the lender. The lender issues a two-party check with the buyer's name and the contractor's name. The HUD inspector has a significant role at each step of the renovation process.

HUD Inspectors Versus Home Inspectors

A standard home inspector can be used instead of a HUD inspector when dealing with a Fannie Mae Homestyle or FHA 203K Limited loan. These reports tend to be a little more challenging to understand, as they are not standardized and subjective. This ultimately can jam up the process, which is why we push to opt for a HUD inspector right from the start. They are the authority and can lead the entire team through the process, providing specificity to the underwriter and not leaving anything up for interpretation. As a real member of the team, a HUD inspector has a larger role than a standard home inspector who is only responsible for providing a report. When the contractor's scope of work is performed, an appraiser will be sent out at the very end to make sure that the proposed repairs were completed and that they appraise out for the particular neighborhood. There could be many gray areas with a home inspector; a HUD inspector will trump an appraiser because the government licenses them. This makes it easy to keep the process clean and efficient. A knowledgeable team with deep renovation lending experience knows exactly what challenges to expect and how to navigate them. When things get bounced back and forth and drag on for months with a team that lacks experience, it's all at the buyer's cost. The expertise of a HUD inspector is invaluable in securing your home and completing the work.

Health and Safety

As contractors, we work closely with HUD inspectors to create a mandatory list of health and safety issues at the property. They have a 35 point checklist of various items that the government deems imperative. Not only does the government want to see these items completed for health and safety purposes, but they also don't want to back a loan without having short-term repairs taken care of. Most people are getting these loans with very little money down. If something like a new roof, septic, or heating system ends up being necessary a couple of years down the road, many of these homes will end up in foreclosure when the homeowners can't afford the repairs. It is best to anticipate what will be needed and include that in the renovation loan. The checklist consists of items such as the following:

The house's envelope must be intact; the roof has to be within five years of its life expectancy, the windows must open and close, and siding cannot be missing. The doors must be operational, and the home needs to be free of trip hazards. There cannot be chipping or peeling paint inside or outside of the house. All mechanicals must be operating, such as water and electricity, and be within three to five years of their life expectancy. When it comes to electrical requirements, there cannot be any knob and tube wiring present in the house. Knob and tube wiring was installed in the early 1900s and is now known to be a fire hazard. Specific electrical panels have been recalled because they don't trip, and the inspector will know which ones to look for. All "wet areas" such as bathrooms or kitchens, must have GFCI outlets. They even go so far as to say there can't be vegetation along the house's exterior within 18 inches, making it necessary for us to go in and cut tree branches that might be hanging over the roof. Leaving the branches can create mold and allow squirrels and other animals to get on or into the house more quickly. Railings are something we commonly install since anything over 28 inches is required to have railings. We see many people who don't even have railings installed properly inside, much less on porches or decks outside the house. People often don't consider these things on their own, making a qualified HUD inspector so important.

Reports

A HUD inspector combined with the right lender is vital when it comes to obtaining required reports. The "Summit" report is a big one that can hinder the process if not completed initially. It is a lead-based paint report and is named after the company contracted out to perform it. It is their job to come out and test every part of the house for lead-based paint. Typically, here in the Northeast, if a house was built in the 1900s, it has lead-based paint, an immediate health and safety issue. If the dust is inhaled or paint chips are consumed, it results in lead poisoning. We often see this come up in the 10th hour near the closing, and it automatically kills the deal, as it can be very costly to do full remediation of an entire home. We can use products that stabilize, neutralize, and encapsulate the paint, running anywhere from $40,000 to $60,000. Since it is such a big undertaking and a crucial health and safety item, the Summit report is imperative so that buyers know what they are getting into. All too often, when we reach the third tier of underwriting and everything is gone through with a fine-tooth comb, these reports surface, and it can be very disheartening for the buyer. Their offer has already been accepted on the property, and the closing is scheduled in a few weeks. Work is expected to begin, and the buyer has already told their landlord they are moving. They then find out the home needs $40,000 of lead paint remediation, and the deal falls apart. It goes back to having the right team of people asking the right questions from the very start.

Let Your Contractor Lead the Way

As a contractor, our training and systems are created around starting the entire renovation loan process with the client and the realtor. When the HUD inspector comes in, we work right alongside him or her to define exactly what the house will require. We form a united front to know exactly what the reports indicate and the necessary items to be completed to meet health and safety standards. We have worked with every HUD inspector in the state of Connecticut, along with some in New York. After a joint walkthrough, we can arm our salespeople with the information necessary to expedite the work. It keeps everyone on the same page and ensures that your home not only turns out the way you want but keeps you and your family safe, happy, and healthy.

Want Our Help?

Claim Your Complimentary "Vision Session" Today!

At Your Vision Session, You Will Discover:

- The best ways to finance your project
- A detailed review of your dream by a highly-trained consultant
- Brainstorming solutions for your project needs
- How we can help you with your dream
- Remodeling industry knowledge shared
- Solutions that fit your "why"

This valuable session is a consultation, not a sales pitch.

Schedule Your Complimentary "Vision Session" at:
www.finehomecontracting.com/book

CHAPTER SIX

Paperwork Pitfalls

The inspections are complete, and everyone is feeling good. To keep the positive momentum going, it is imperative not to get caught up in the trap of paperwork and scope of work, which is where a lot of inexperienced contractors start to slip. This portion is significant for the lender because they are selling the loan, which ultimately ends up being backed by the government. The government has particular expectations. A good lender/contractor team will know how to process and package the paperwork so that it doesn't get kicked back during the underwriting process.

The underwriter will first examine the health and safety items listed on the original reports, comparing them to the HUD or home inspection reports.

They will read the contractor's scope of work to make sure that each item has been completed. Also, they are looking for material and labor breakdowns from the contractor and 35 specific categories that the HUD inspector is responsible for addressing. Everything needs to align and be relatively easy for office personnel to make sense of. When a HUD inspector is involved, they produce 20-30 pages of documentation, including the scope of work, legal contracts, wishlist items, and required permits. Even after underwriting, the appraiser will need to look over everything again to determine how the work will raise the property value. In an industry where we see many guys in trucks handing out quotes on napkins or the back of business cards, the paperwork is undoubtedly the most significant area of friction. We have streamlined the process with templates and management software, worked with every lender out there, and even so, it takes our sales team hours to put the paperwork together. Tripping points can occur every step of the way. Without a clear scope of work and organized documentation, it will delay the entire process and prevent you from getting to the fun part...your wishlist items and to the closing table! Choosing a knowledgeable contractor and lender will result in legible scopes of work and a smooth, stress-free underwriting experience.

Once the paperwork package has been submitted to the lender, it goes to underwriting. If everything checks out, the appraisal happens. This is the last step of the process, typically occurring within a week or two of closing. The appraiser uses a system of checks and balances to ensure that you are increasing value while not over-improving for your particular neighborhood. Sometimes an appraiser will go through and find things that the HUD inspector or home inspector missed. For example, they may find a broken window in the basement. If this happens, the whole scope of work needs to be re-done, and sometimes it can push the prices up enough that the client can no longer afford the loan. We consider ourselves experts in the field, and one of our primary goals is to get our clients to the finish line and into their new home. When the inspectors miss items, we take it upon ourselves to put it into our contract and take care of it regardless.

Real estate transactions are known to be high-paced and stressful. When you add in the additional required elements of a renovation loan, the skill level of the team of people you have working for you is even more crucial. If one box isn't checked, if one "t" isn't crossed, it can be devastating for the buyer, realtor, and loan officer. Most people already have an offer on their previous home at the paperwork stage and are gearing up to move in a couple of weeks. They are maxed out on their mortgage and will be forced to walk away if significant items were overlooked along the way. The last thing we want is for deals to fall apart because of items being missed. We do everything in our power to make sure that doesn't happen. This is an added benefit of working with a team of people who not only understand the "power of paperwork" but have your best interest and homeownership goals in mind.

Want Our Help?

Claim Your Complimentary "Vision Session" Today!

At Your Vision Session, You Will Discover:

- The best ways to finance your project
- A detailed review of your dream by a highly-trained consultant
- Brainstorming solutions for your project needs
- How we can help you with your dream
- Remodeling industry knowledge shared
- Solutions that fit your "why"

This valuable session is a consultation, not a sales pitch.

Schedule Your Complimentary "Vision Session" at:

www.finehomecontracting.com/book

CHAPTER SEVEN

The Loan Door Closes; The Work Window Opens

T he action starts happening once the closing has taken place and the loan is funded.
The customer receives a "welcome package"
from the lender, detailing how the contractors will
receive payment and getting everyone on the same
page. The loan typically closes within one week
of its scheduled time, at which point we mobilize.
Our Project Manager, salesperson, and customer
meet to go over, line by line, the items that have
been sold. This immediately flushes out any mis-
understandings or miscommunications. They will
discuss the entire contract and scope of work. For
example, "We're doing 10 feet of linear cabinets in
the kitchen, a new roof with 50-year shingles, Pella

windows, and vinyl siding everywhere except the garage." This ensures that the project's interpretation is correct, and any questions or concerns that the buyer has will be addressed at this time.

Project Prep

The way we handle project prep is taken from processes that are commonly used in the commercial space. We don't start work until we have bought out and scheduled the entire project. We send out purchase orders to every subcontractor, have them look at the scope of work, and meet at the property. The goal is to have everybody in contract with the costs all lined up, so we hit our budget before the actual work begins.

From there, everything is broken down into what we refer to as a "Gantt" schedule. Henry Gantt invented this bar chart in 1910 that clearly illustrates a project schedule. Each company will agree upon specific dates when they will get their part of the project done. The nice thing about the Gnatt software is that we can enter contractors in real-time. If the plumber will be there for three days, and the electrician needs to overlap, we can illustrate that.

If they both have to be done by Friday because the drywall comes on Monday, the software will automatically notify them in their purchase orders. The Project Manager can adjust the schedule by dragging one bar on the chart, at which point all of the preceding contractors will be notified by email that they have been bumped one day. This keeps everyone on task and keeps the process rolling, even in the event of a hiccup since, inevitably, things happen no matter how organized you are. Powerful automated software makes everyone's lives a lot easier.

Our Project Manager oversees all of this, adding cushion days here and there and making sure everything adds up. We also have a Production Manager reviewing purchase orders and dates as the second set of eyes. They will alert the team of any red flags or things that may have been overlooked, such as, "You missed the countertop installation. Where can we fit that in?"

Demos and special orders can back everything up. We find it beneficial to get all of our special orders onsite before we even demo. For example, we will order the kitchen cabinets, inspect them for damage, and confirm sizing so that when it is time to pull the trigger, we are good to go. As we move through the prep process, the city is also involved, pulling permits and approving plans. This is why it is essential to communicate to the customer that even though we know they are excited for work to begin, patience is required during these first couple of weeks of project prep. Though they may not be seeing physical work being performed yet, a lot goes on behind the scenes as far as pre-planning on our software, scheduling vendors, and making sure each contractor knows when to show up.

One thing that can keep the customer busy while the project is being prepped is visiting our partner showrooms to choose the home's exact pieces, such as toilets, faucets, flooring, and the specific corresponding colors. We already have these items broken into three different cost tiers. We coordinate with the sales reps who will show the customer the ten faucets available within their allowance to choose from. These finishing choices are important to get nailed down right away, especially in the event of a special order or discontinued item so that nobody is sitting around waiting once work begins.

Permits

In the project prep time frame, permits must also be pulled before work starts. This is a time in the process where we can be thrown curveballs, and have devoted a lot of our time and continuing education to dealing with permit issues. Even though there is a title search done before closing and attorneys need to do their research to determine there are no outstanding liens on the property, we have often come across the situation of open permits. This means that someone did work on the home previously and never had it inspected. We will then be required to have the inspector come out and close the permits before opening new ones. Some friction can occur here since each town has different requirements. Each building inspector can read the code and come up with something completely different. Coding is not as cut and dry as most people think. Just like the law, it is open to interpretation, which is why we have attorneys and judges. The same goes for building inspectors. New codes come out, and they haven't educated themselves, so they interpret it a certain way and mandate us to do certain things that we weren't prepared for. This may slow the project's progress as we readjust our plans. For example, we see it a lot when it comes to insulation in older homes. Some inspectors will say, "It appears you have put as much insulation in the wall as you can with the current framing." Others will say, "You need to bring this up to code. Your wall cavities aren't big enough, and you need to upgrade to spray foam." Then we need to figure out a new plan of action. We make our customers aware that small issues like this can come up during the permit process. Fortunately for us, our name is out there, and the building departments know us well. Most of the time, they don't beat us up as much as they could.

Another example would involve inspections taking place on-site while we are already doing the work. We can be working on a kitchen on the first floor, and the inspector goes into the basement and finds an old water heater that was not installed correctly ten years ago. Because it is a health and safety issue, they will require it to be fixed before continuing our work. This is a tough conversation to have with the customer because we can't leave, and they have to pay for it. The town doesn't want the liability of the house burning down, and we need to be released of that permit so that we are not liable for anything going wrong with the water heater. We have a lot of experience talking customers through these circumstances and helping them make decisions that will allow work to continue safely. We value continuing education for all of our employees to handle any situation during the permit process with knowledge and professionalism.

Utilities

Since the housing crisis of 2008, which involved thousands and thousands of foreclosures, utilities are a tricky thing to deal with, even still. Banks were overwhelmed and had no idea what to do. So they just shut off the utilities to all of these foreclosures, the pipes burst, and it was just a mess. 203K loans work very well with these types of foreclosed homes, and we still come across the ones where everything has been turned off. We often don't know what we are getting into. Over the past couple of years, things have gotten better to the point where some banks will pay to get things pressure tested. But each bank handles things differently, so we generally have to take a completely different route when we run into homes with utilities that have been shut down. Our goal is to get water running, electricity on, and heating systems going before anything else starts. Most of the time, we end up replacing everything. For example, we came across a home with city water that had been turned off for six years, and the main water line coming into the house had eroded to the point where it needed to be replaced. Nobody before us was able to figure that out. It was a considerable cost. Fortunately, we found it right up front during the project and were able to reallocate funds from a bathroom to get the new line installed. The moral of the story...priority number one is getting utilities up and running. Our customers using renovation loans generally don't have that much extra cash laying around. We can't just ask them for an additional $20,000 that isn't there. Once the loan is closed, you would have to rewrite the whole mortgage to get any more money from the bank. That is why it is crucial to have an experienced team who can quickly identify these issues and find ways to move money around effectively to cover hidden costs.

Progress Reports

Once the work begins, it is very fast-paced, organized, and detailed, which results from all those prep work hours. First, a porta-potty, dumpster, and hand washing station get delivered. The construction team will go into the home and plastic wall areas to be worked on, sealing other living areas from the dust and debris. Step by step, the demolition begins. Once the demo is complete, we take a slight pause and reevaluate. Upon opening walls, sometimes we will find rot or structural elements that have been compromised. At that point, we might have to do a change order where we go into the contingency fund and say we need to perform this additional work to get back up to code. It often takes a couple of days for everyone, including the homeowner and HUD consultant, to sit down and sign off on the new work, ensuring they understand safety and liability issues. Then, once again, the work takes off at a fast pace. Our Project Manager gives a weekly progress report, which we have found to be very beneficial. They sit down with the client and go over, step by step, the work that has been performed that week. They discuss things like workmanship and whether or not the client is happy with their choices. If there are any discrepancies, everything is documented and uploaded into our system. By catching issues as they arise, we avoid any problems at the end of the job. If something wasn't installed correctly, we could get the appropriate contractor back quickly instead of trying to track them down three to four weeks down the road. Attention to detail and proper project preparation time takes the stress out of the demo stage as the transformation of your home begins to take shape.

Want Our Help?

Claim Your Complimentary "Vision Session" Today!

At Your Vision Session, You Will Discover:

- The best ways to finance your project
- A detailed review of your dream by a highly-trained consultant
- Brainstorming solutions for your project needs
- How we can help you with your dream
- Remodeling industry knowledge shared
- Solutions that fit your "why"

This valuable session is a consultation, not a sales pitch.

Schedule Your Complimentary "Vision Session" at:

www.finehomecontracting.com/book

CHAPTER EIGHT

The Long-Awaited, Highly-Anticipated, Renovation Project

O nce the demo is complete, the home starts buzzing with action. The new floor plan is taking shape, windows are being placed, and the whole project starts to come to life. However, we still leave room for flexibility when meeting the client's needs and wants. Perhaps during a weekly progress report meeting, the homeowner mentions wanting to make some slight changes. It may be as simple as finding different fixtures or finishes that they like better or as complex as changing some walls around in the floor plan's framing. Either way, we strive to make everyone happy. For many of our clients, they plan on creating their "forever home." Their satisfaction takes priority over anything else, which is why we allow for change orders.

Change orders, when done incorrectly, are one of the biggest reasons projects go south. They must be done in real-time with true costs that are continually added and paid for upfront. We have seen contractors who issue a $50,000 change order at the very end of a project that the customer doesn't have the money for or wasn't even aware of! This is one of the reasons construction courts exist. The contractor puts a lien on the house, and the whole thing ends very badly. We take every step necessary to ensure our customers never have this experience. The minute we are veering away from our original work scope or contract, we sit down and have a meeting. Anything over $500 is an automatic change order and is gone over in detail with the Project Manager and the client. Our software makes for a smooth process, as the Project Manager can take out his iPad and create the change order in real-time with photos and a detailed breakdown. Even if not present in person, the client can quickly sign off on the change, which triggers an invoice added to their total project amount.

Unforeseen events can also result in change orders. For example, we may be tearing up a bathroom floor, and nobody realized the tub had been leaking. A change order would be created to replace the subfloor. With any renovation project, there are situations like this that simply can't be predicted ahead of time.

Contingency Fund

The contingency fund is a reserve of money set aside as part of the loan to be used for unforeseen circumstances such as those discussed above. It essentially acts as a safety net to cover issues that present themselves during the demo phase or forgotten or overlooked during the planning stages. Let's face it; we're all human and should be allowed that margin of error. As a company, we understand that we will inevitably need to allocate those funds to large projects. We might not always know precisely where in the beginning stages, but as the project progresses and things come up, the team can meet and determine where the money is best used. The contingency fund is 10% to 15%, so on a big project totaling $200,000, there could be $20,000 in funds. The data that HUD has collected concludes that most projects are off by about 10%. For renovation loans, the customer would want to use this money, as it won't add to their monthly payment.

Even with this fund acting as a cushion, contractors must be extremely accurate in their sales process. We have seen contractors go in, toss a number out there, and think they will get more money once they get in the door. It simply doesn't work that way. The renovation portion of the mortgage gets put into an escrow account. Once that account is empty, there is no more money to get on the back end. Our team carefully calculates everything from the start to ensure the project is funded entirely and efficiently.

Progress Payments

At this point, you may be wondering how the crews doing all of the manual labor receive payment. For full 203K or Homestyle Loans and any project totaling over $35,000, an inspection company or HUD inspector will be on the scene to guide the payment process. We generally work in $25,000 increments, calculated in percentages. For example, we may hit $25,000 by completing 100% of the roof, 50% of the windows, and 10% of the flooring. The HUD consultant or inspection company, depending on the lender, will inspect the completed work. They take photos, gather copies of our permits, and have us sign lien waivers. Each subcontractor must sign a lien waiver, which indicates that they have received payment in the agreed-upon amount and will not walk off the job. It is very easy for contractors to claim they didn't get paid and put a lien on the property. Though lien waivers are typically seen in commercial construction, we have implemented them across the board to protect our customers from any subcontractor they may be working with. The customer will also sign off to express their agreement. This entire paperwork package is then submitted to the lender for approval and release of funds. The lender typically sends us a two-part check with our name and the homeowner's name. The homeowner signs the back of the check, and we can deposit it. Since we do a lot of work and are familiar with many lenders, we can also request a wire transfer to be deposited directly into our account. This eliminates the possibility of a UPS envelope sitting on the doorstep of a vacant house containing a check for $80,000. The only thing that does is stress everyone out!

David Perrotti

As change orders reach completion and the progress payments stack, your new home is just within reach. The final stretch is fast approaching!

Want Our Help?

Claim Your Complimentary "Vision Session" Today!

At Your Vision Session, You Will Discover:

- The best ways to finance your project
- A detailed review of your dream by a highly-trained consultant
- Brainstorming solutions for your project needs
- How we can help you with your dream
- Remodeling industry knowledge shared
- Solutions that fit your "why"

This valuable session is a consultation, not a sales pitch.

Schedule Your Complimentary "Vision Session" at:
www.finehomecontracting.com/book

CHAPTER NINE

Crossing the Finish Line

L ike most runners toward the end of a race, the whole team might be a little tired as we approach the finish line. The last phase of the project is typically when the most issues arise, including damaged special order items, delays, and homeowners who are tired of decision making and just want to move in already. If the client has been living in the home during the renovation, they are undoubtedly ready for everyone to be out. Our Production Manager takes special care to interject some positive energy into the whole group, understanding people's psychology being tired and anxious for completion.

We also change the way we work at this point. Half of the fixtures, floors, and other items are new now, so we take extra precautions to protect what is there while installing appliances, countertops, etc. Heavy-duty checklists and procedures encompass this portion of the work, as we check in with the customer more frequently, going over punch list items line by line, room by room. We make sure that everyone feels work has been completed satisfactorily. Undoubtedly, we will have customers who are not 100% happy with some of their choices, but we do our best to keep up the energy and keep the project moving. Though that pink countertop choice may be driving them crazy at the moment, everyone always feels a lot better about things once they are officially moved in.

Final Inspections

Once the work is complete, the city comes in to do its final inspection. If it was a "one inspection" project, this might be the first time the city has been on the property. They have the right to point out any health and safety issues still present. As much as we educate ourselves and stay up-to-date on codes, sometimes a brand new one is sprung on us in these final stages, and we must roll with it. For example, in the state of Connecticut right now, if you pull a building permit, they will not close it out unless all brand new smoke and carbon monoxide detectors have been installed in homes with combustion heating sources. The existing ones must not be older than ten years. Smoke detectors save lives, so there is no leniency when it comes to this topic. We have learned to put this in the very beginning of our contract now, to avoid issues at the end. Since it can be a $1,000 to $1,500 cost in larger homes, customers appreciate not being blindsided by that cost as well.

It is essential to choose contractors savvy to new codes and how they differ from city to city, especially when it comes to electrical, plumbing, and HVAC. Having open permits can leave you stuck with a property, which we often see in real estate. Mortgage companies will not fund loans on properties with open permits. Contractors must understand that they can even be held responsible for health and safety items that had nothing to do with them. For example, during the final inspection, the city might go down to the basement to check out a new electrical box we installed. On the way, they pass by the water heater and discover it is not bonded or has a safety release valve that is not working correctly. Even though the water heater has been there for 15 years, it is a potential fire hazard. We now need to fix it for the permit to be closed out. Otherwise, the city could be sued for negligence.

Once the home passes the city inspection, all items have been fixed, and permits are closed out, the lender inspection occurs. The final lender inspection will be done by either the HUD consultant, inspection company, or an appraiser. They want to see proof that the permits have been closed out and that the customer is happy with the completed work. The lender inspection revolves more around the customer experience than the health and safety concerns of the city. The lender assembles the final draw payment paperwork and does a title search on the property to confirm that no liens have been issued by contractors working on the home. Once that is clear, the final payment is given plus the 10% they have held back on every other draw payment throughout the project. That portion is held to keep the contractors accountable and ensures they finish the project properly. When hiring a contractor, they must be well-capitalized since they have to fund and buy the project before getting paid. It can be difficult for smaller companies to float money throughout the process, but it is necessary for this business.

Project Completion

We do quite a bit of paperwork in house, with the primary goal of making our company better with each project. Upon completion, we have specific punch lists that we go over with the customer and grill them on their overall experience, ensuring they were satisfied each step of the way and what we could improve upon.

Additionally, we sit down and have a full job review with the entire team, including the Production Manager, salesperson, and Project Manager. We ask key questions such as, "Did we complete the project on schedule? Did we stay within budget? Did the customer give us a five-star review? What wasn't clear to the customer? Can we change some of our specs and selections?" At the end of this meeting, we come up with two or three actionable steps to improve our services. We make updates right away, so the next job starts with better verbiage in the contract or new specs that will make the entire customer experience more enjoyable. I believe this is the reason why our success is so constant. We never stop learning from constructive criticism and adapting, which has become increasingly vital during the recent pandemic and continues to propel our mission to give people beautiful, comfortable homes.

Want Our Help?

Claim Your Complimentary "Vision Session" Today!

At Your Vision Session, You Will Discover:

- The best ways to finance your project
- A detailed review of your dream by a highly-trained consultant
- Brainstorming solutions for your project needs
- How we can help you with your dream
- Remodeling industry knowledge shared
- Solutions that fit your "why"

This valuable session is a consultation, not a sales pitch.

Schedule Your Complimentary "Vision Session" at:
www.finehomecontracting.com/book

CHEERS TO YOUR DREAM HOME...

Your home is your castle. It is not only your most significant investment, but the place you will spend the most time and create lasting memories with your family. When you step through that front door, it should simply make you feel good, whether peaceful or energetic. A remodel is often the key to unlocking those feelings. Renovation loans bring accessibility to the average person to achieve the remodel of their dreams. As we have discussed, there are many ins and outs and professionals involved in the process. But don't let that scare you away. Do your research, assemble a quality team, and have FUN. Imagine how good that new home office, updated kitchen, or additional space will make you feel. And remember that renovation loans are the cheapest and most valuable way to remodel because you are rolling it into your mortgage, getting you everything you have always wanted with a low monthly payment. With a little planning, a little grit, and a little decision making with your team, you will be sitting and enjoying that new space with your family in no time.

David Perrotti

ABOUT DAVID PERROTTI

President and Founder
Fine Home Contracting LLC

David Perrotti grew up in Connecticut and was raised in a lower-middle-class family. His father was a mechanic, and his mother cleaned houses. At the age of 15, he followed in the footsteps of many of his friends and began working part-time for a carpentry company performing most of the "grunt work" and cleanup duties through a work-study program at his high school. He has been passionate about the trades ever since.

In 2001, upon graduating, David joined the military for patriotic reasons and saw an opportunity there.

He was quickly deployed to Iraq and did his first tour from 2002 to 2003. After about 18 months, he immediately jumped back into the trades. He continued to hone his carpenter skills, from framing houses to installing doors, windows, siding, and hardwood floors.

He was deployed to Iraq once more in 2008 and came back to find a broken economy. Housing prices had fallen apart, and the company he had been working for was nearly out of business. He found himself out of a job. David decided to take the GI Bill and get his Business Management Degree from the University of Connecticut. The school prepared him for a "cubicle" job in business, but David just couldn't wrap his head around that. He was used to being out in the field swinging a hammer or active military duty and didn't connect with the corporate environment.

So, like any guy starting out on his own, David took his hammer and his beat-up van and decided to go into business for himself. He had all of this experience in the trades and now knew how to run a company. Doing jobs for family and friends, completing quality work, and scaling from there, David's mission was to set a standard in the home remodeling industry. Sure, many companies were trying to be the big guys in remodeling, but they focused on the trades and neglected the business and customer service aspects. David knew his customers deserved open lines of communication, detailed estimates, management of expectations, and adherence to schedules and budgets. Most of the guys out there could tear apart a kitchen and install a new one, but the customer experience was not great along the way. With his customer service mission and the acquisition of excellent business management software, David has elevated the remodeling industry standards as President of Fine Home Contracting LLC to meet customers' needs throughout Connecticut.

He often tells his team that it is their mission to reinvent the remodeling experience. Every project is evaluated not only on the quality of work performed and pricing but how the overall customer experience can be improved. After all, home renovation is a substantial investment. Elevating industry standards is of utmost importance to David and his team at Fine Home Contracting LLC, simply because their customers deserve it.

EMAIL:
Info@finehomecontracting.com

PHONE:
860-733-2080

FACEBOOK:
https://www.facebook.com/finehomecontracting

YOUTUBE:
https://www.youtube.com/channel/
UC0UPEOLE2ixebQEXMy0SLyw

INSTAGRAM:
https://www.instagram.com/finehomecontracting/

PINTEREST:
h t t p s : / / p i n t e r e s t . c o m /
Finehomecontracting/_created/

LINKEDIN:
https://www.linkedin.com/company/
fine-home-contracting-llc

TWITTER:
https://twitter.com/DavidPerrotti

WHAT DAVID'S CLIENTS ARE SAYING

Positive:
Professionalism, Punctuality, Quality, Responsiveness, Value

My wife Michelle would rate our experience with Fine Home Contracting a 10 out of 10! We are so happy with the way our kitchen remodel came out. Our project manager Fred Adkins was so great as well as everyone on his crew. Everyone was so professional, friendly, respected our home and pets, and we can't say enough of how happy we are. We LOVED the free online tool we were given called Co-Contruct which outlines Every Penny and Every step of the process from start to finish. It is evident to us that Fine Home and it's crew care about it's customers and doing everything the right way. I can't imagine using anyone else for anything home related. We highly recommend them and LOVE our new kitchen.

-Michael Ormsby

We used Fine Home Contracting LLC to put an addition on our master bedroom. We would highly recommend them to anyone and if we ever decide to add on or do any large home maker over projects wouldn't hesitate to hire them again. They were always professional and courteous, and always let us know when someone would be coming ahead of time. Anytime I had a question no matter how small, it was always answered in a very timely manner.

-Melissa Hine

I recently purchased a home with a 203k loan and I used Fine Home Contracting to do the repair work. My experience was very pleasant. Words can't express how easy it was to deal with them. The work they did on my home was immaculate. True professionals.

-Marvin Kelly III

Dave and his crew recently finished a 203k project on our first home we bought as a foreclosure. There was a ton of work to be done and we went through a nightmare of a loan process, but as soon as the papers were signed in Dave made us feel at ease and over-delivered every step of the way. Not only did he complete all the jobs sooner than we expected, he kept us up to date and asked for our opinion every step of the way, and delivered craftsman quality. I would recommend Fine Home Contracting for any home improvement needs, but especially for new homeowners looking for an honest contractor.

-Chelsea Lynn Spencer

My wife and I took a chance on a HUD owned property and hired Dave as our general contractor. Dave's understanding of the 203K renovation process and his relationships in the field helped ensure a quick and easy project. Dave and his team were very helpful with options to upgrade our home and was very flexible when we changed up our plan. The quality of workmanship and professionalism was much appreciated and I highly recommend hiring Dave if you decide to venture into a Reno project of your own. Thanks Dave for all your help. We love our new home!

-Jamie Sauvageua